Discover God's Unconditional Love

Color, Journal, and Pray Through the Pain Using Essential Oils

Melanie Rose Schroeder Saccomanno

Copyright © 2019 Melanie Rose Schroeder Saccomanno
Illustrations and design @2019 Melanie Rose Schroeder Saccomanno

All rights reserved. No part of this book may be reproduced or transmitted in any form or by any means, including but not limited to information storage and retrieval systems, electronic, mechanical, photocopy, recording, etc. without expressed written consent of the author.

Scripture quotations from The Authorized (King James) Version. Rights in the Authorized Version in the United Kingdom are vested in the Crown. Reproduced by permission of the Crown's patentee, Cambridge University Press.

Scripture quotations are from The ESV® Bible (The Holy Bible, English Standard Version®), copyright © 2001 by Crossway, a publishing ministry of Good News Publishers. Used by permission. All rights reserved.

Scripture quotations marked (NIV) are taken from the Holy Bible, New International Version®, NIV®. Copyright © 1973, 1978, 1984, 2011 by Biblica, Inc.™ Used by permission of Zondervan. All rights reserved worldwide. www.zondervan.com The "NIV" and "New International Version" are trademarks registered in the United States Patent and Trademark Office by Biblica, Inc.™

Scripture taken from the New King James Version®. Copyright © 1982 by Thomas Nelson. Used by permission. All rights reserved.

Edited and formatted by Ascribe Communications, Columbus, Ohio
ISBN: 9781698843605

ACKNOWLEDGMENTS

There are so many people I want to thank for helping me move forward with this book.

First of all, I thank my Father in Heaven for giving me the Holy Spirit and the ability to draw. Little did I know what He was really doing as I created picture pages during painful times of feeling heavy or scattered.

Secondly, I thank my family and especially my husband, Peter, who endured a messy home strewn with art supplies, books, and Bibles for many days. Your patience and support were invaluable to me as I waited for inspiration and vision to walk through this journey of focusing on the kingdom of God and His purposes for our trials and victories.

Thirdly, I must mention my mom and dad, Papa Don and Mama Gail Schroeder. Thank you, Dad, for telling me that I can do anything and encouraging me to be a better person. Mom, witnessing your overcoming faith and your passion to know Jesus and the power of His resurrection has been a great influence in my life. You have helped me to see that it isn't how we start the race, but how we finish it that counts. You have a legacy of "amazing grace," and God is using you to teach this generation what you have learned through the cares and trials of your life. Thank you, Mom and Dad!

Last but certainly not least, I want to…
- Thank Olive Baptist Church for years of love and discipleship;
- Give a huge shout out to Jubilee International for helping me to find my "voice" again;
- Thank Mama Hugs and Abundant Life Ministries for years of training me about soul healing;
- Thank Donna Partow, founder of Women's Empowerment University and her partner, Tamara Aragon, in Lifestyle Freedom, Costa Rico 2019, for encouraging me to move forward in my purpose and passions;
- Give a big hug to Kristin Reeg and Ascribe Communications for helping me to become an author.

Doodle Page

PREFACE

This is an art journal. I believe new doors will open for you as you read, color, and doodle. Do you ever feel like you are so busy that you can't slow down? Is your to-do list overwhelming? Maybe you are trying to create space for fun and relaxation in your life. Whatever your motive, you are in for a real treat from our Heavenly Father. As you learn to *just BE* and color, you will give your brain room to breathe. Let your mind stop wandering and focus on resting and creating in Him. Peace will come.

Does this sound challenging? Do you feel as though the darkness and heaviness of life has anchored your soul? During my stressful times, the Holy Spirit would bring to light something in my heart. He taught me to just write it down—whatever it was. I was okay to admit how I was feeling—even if those emotions were full of sorrow or anger. Daddy God is so gentle and refreshing. All stress departs in His presence. My prayer is that you will experience the Word and discover new gifts in you for His glory.

Truth be told, I didn't know I was an artist. I was always in trouble for doodling as a child. I was often chastised for speaking too much, being too loud, and asking too many questions. Is that you, one of your friends, or even your child? I began to dislike who I was because I was corrected or criticized constantly. As I pursue a relationship with Jesus, I find the hidden joy in my struggles from childhood until now. Jesus always loves me. He is never harsh; He is gentle with my thoughts and emotions. He is always getting me where I need to be. Life is full of challenges, but I have found true freedom in my Author and Perfecter. Jesus keeps drawing me to HIM; Christ in me is my only HOPE. I pray that you, too, will find that Jesus is your hope. I believe that your true identity will come forth as you count the cost. There is always a cost for freedom; nevertheless, it is always worth it. **Letting go is freedom.**

Amazing Grace was my late brother Michael's favorite movie. His hand was so manly, yet so tender, as he held mine as we unknowingly watched it together for the last time. He and Little Jerry and other loved ones are cheering on my family from heaven. God has carried us through much grief and pain. Part of this journal was birthed by allowing God to walk me through those valleys of sorrow. God took me through the valley and up the next mountain. I found joy again; you can too.

I pray you choose joy in the journey regardless of the struggle. I pray gifts you haven't even tapped into will be released as you run this race with diligence and fulfill your destiny until you are called home to Heaven. Intimacy with Jesus is always the perfect destination.

Press into God as you Himtangle with your Daddy God. He has great things in store for you. He is not challenged by your lack. He wants to allow your deficits to come forth as you depend on HIM daily and use your gifts to glorify Him.

"The joy of the Lord is your strength, hold your peace,... neither be ye grieved" (Nehemiah 8:10-11 KJV).

Doodle Page

INTRODUCTION

Have you ever had days like this? Days when everything in your body hurts. Days when staying in bed is a more appealing option than going through the daily routine. I have 40 days until my late brother, Michael Schroeder's birthday and Valentine's Day. Nevertheless, I am choosing to press through because I want to see what God can do despite the battle. I want to believe with you for breakthrough in your struggles! God wants to be the solution when you are faced with an obstacle. God put a message in my heart, and I want to extract the message from the pain.

For the last six years, my life has been much death, loss, pain, sickness in family, caregiving, and nurturing. Himtangle came as a result of my reflections with God. He met me as I drew and focused on the word He gave me or the picture I saw. God is so sweet; He was healing my heart in the doodle, in the coloring, and in the water coloring. As I experienced His love, my heart and head connected.

My prayer for you as you draw, pray, and ponder what may be hindering you from dreaming or growing is that you will be amazed by the majesty of the Father for YOU. Yes, you! He loves you and all you are NOT. May you be overwhelmed by the love of God as you allow Holy Spirit to massage your heart. Rest in the Father's affection for you! He is your perfection! **He so loves YOU!** His mercies are new every morning, and He turns our mourning into joy.

As you travel through these pages, ENJOY the journey. God wants us to live in a childlike faith. He is always in color. NO more black and white, but a rainbow! Choose to see the world in living color TODAY. Joy comes by rejoicing in WHO you are in Christ, not WHAT you lack. May you embrace this challenge to allow Christ, the Son of the Living God, to mold you into His image. Embrace the artist inside of you. God created the world and YOU. There is an artist inside of YOU. As you color your world around you, let the Father speak to your heart.

Every day is a gift. Our Heavenly Father is the perfect lover of your soul. Allow Him to have all of you. He can be trusted.

Rest in Daddy God's love for you.

Doodle Page

HIMTANGLE Preparation

Create in me a clean heart, O God, and renew a right spirit within me.
Psalm 51:10 ESV

What You'll Need
Drawing art materials, colored pencils, sketchbook or color page
Bible or other texts of poetry, or nature

BASIC STEPS FOR EMOTIONAL RELEASE WHEN COLORING

1. Be still and close your eyes. Be aware of how you feel, take in a few deep breaths, and ask yourself what you are concerned about.

2. Let go of what is weighing you down. See yourself handing that concern, person, or emotion to God.

3. Focus on God and who He is and reflect on all He has done for you.

4. Ask God to give you a greater awareness of His presence, greater vision, and imagery.

5. Be open and listen to your heart.

6. When you are ready pick up your tool and begin coloring, let go of control and let God lead.

7. When finished coloring or drawing, look at your artwork, and write what you hear the Lord saying to you regarding the picture or scripture you interpreted.

8. Don't push your own ideas. It is not about good artwork; it is about listening to the Lord and responding using a visual art.

THERE ARE NO MISTAKES IN ART.

This book is a perfect gift for all who are physically (so much on the to-do list), emotionally (trying to figure it all out), and spiritually (needing refreshed) exhausted.

May you find **BALANCE** and **FREEDOM** in body, soul, and spirit.

DOODLE **P**AGE

WHAT IS HIMTANGLE?

Himtangle is doodle art with a message. After losing two younger brothers in a short period of time, I found myself doodling my pastor's sermons into art. Himtangle came out of my personal journey from grief, despair, and confusion to rest and real joy in my soul.

My desire for these coloring pages is to help you untangle your emotions and draw closer to God. Each page has a message and comes with an optional devotional and journaling prompt for those times when coloring is not enough!

Color your heart out and discover the artist in you!!!

> You can do all things IN Christ who gives you strength.
> Philippians 4:13 paraphrased

Doodle Page

THE BLEEDING HEART

We love because he first loved us.
1 John 4:19 NIV

For God so loved the world that he gave his one and only Son,
that whoever believes in him shall not perish but have eternal life.
John 3:16 NIV

Casting down imaginations, and every high thing that exalteth itself against the
knowledge of God, and bringing into captivity every thought to the obedience of Christ.
2 Corinthians 10:5 KJV

Do you feel like you have a bleeding heart?

Have you said you don't want the pain anymore?

Are you numb, unable to feel the pain, because the pain is too unbearable? Let this be your go to page. Ask Holy Spirit what subtle lies you have believed. It is the lies we believe that cause our hearts to ache. As we embrace what we are thinking, we are able to change the emotions that have shut down that area of our beautiful hearts. You **can** and **will** love once again. Our thoughts can be very toxic if we do not take them captive. Remember, God loves you unconditionally—without restraint.

Do you think God is harsh?

Do you believe God can and will do what He says He will do?

Don't be afraid to write down your answers here. Note what comes to you around the empty white space on your coloring page. God already knows these feelings exist. As you write them, you expose them; darkness has to flee. Your heart is precious to Jesus; He is patiently waiting and loving you through this process.

The Heart of Jesus for You
I am drawing you to Myself because this isn't the life I have in store for you. Allow Me to massage your heart, and know that I have your back in every situation. I am your vindicator, and I am fighting for you. Look to Me in the pain. I am here for you always. I never left you. I am singing over you with shouts of joy. I see no flaws in you. (Exodus 14:14; Zephaniah 3:17; Song of Solomon 7:4)

CREATE IN ME

Take a few minutes to be still and meditate on what is on your heart.

How are you feeling today? The heart is the seat of our emotions. It governs our behavior every day. As you look at this tangled heart, begin to reflect on your thoughts and write down those areas in YOUR heart. Start with the positive thoughts that you think that are pleasing to the Lord, then address those areas you want Holy Spirit to change. God isn't going to condemn you. He already knows what you are thinking. He is so pleased you are willing to share your heart with Him.

King David wrote Psalm 51 after he had sinned with Bathsheba. "Purge me with hyssop, and I shall be clean; wash me, and I shall be whiter than snow.... Cast me not away from your presence, and take not your Holy Spirit from me. Restore to me the joy of your salvation, and uphold me with a willing spirit" (vs. 7,11-12).

As you sit in the presence of the Lord and meditate on this word, healing and freedom will come. Write in the area below a prayer in your own words. David was grieving, and during those days essential oils were used in all areas of their lives. Today, hyssop is used for respiratory support. How amazing! God created oils with His breath; even today, they can be used for healing. *Healing Oils of the Bible* by Dr. Stewart is an amazing reference if you are interested in learning more about the benefits of oils and the science behind them. The JOY oil is also available for heart health and emotional balancing when life hits you with those hard knocks. The link to order is: https://www.myyl.com/msaccomanno.

Keep seeking the Lord and focus on Him—not circumstances. Spending time with Him will keep your heart pliable, passionate, and able to love Him with your whole heart.

<u>Prayer</u>
Jesus, I give you my heart. Heal it, and make it whole. I thank You for being available to me. Help me to trust You with my whole heart. Mold me into Your image. Holy Spirit, come speak to me and show me Your truths.

DREAMY HEART: BELIEVE AND AWAKEN

All things are possible for one who believes .
Mark 9:23 ESV

*If any of you lacks wisdom, you should ask God, who gives generously
to all without finding fault, and it will be given to you*
James 1:5 NIV

Are you a dreamer, or have you stopped dreaming?

It is important to ask Holy Spirit what His intentions are for you daily! He has a good plan. Consider writing down all those things you want to see happen in your life. Ask God what His dreams are for you. As you ask, He will give you a strategy one step at a time. Your dreams are God's intentions for you. He just wants to be in charge. When your dreams don't manifest immediately, does that make you doubt yourself sometimes? I know I've struggled with doubt. But, guess what? God's timing is perfect. You are in God's waiting room learning to wait but with purpose.

Believe™ Young Living oil is amazing for when you need to repent, embrace all the promises of God, and stand on His word. The oils change cellular memory and support the nervous system to bring you back into harmony.

Awaken™ is a perfect oil to diffuse as well. It helps to awaken any area in your life where you feel dry or even numb. Be open and be expecting God to answer your tender heart. He is always waiting to bestow good gifts on His children. As a parent, we want to bless our children. How much more does our Heavenly Father want to bless us?

Refuse to let logic interfere with what Holy Spirit wants to do. You don't have to figure it all out. It will only wear you out—take it from me! I love to connect the dots, but many times understanding comes from simple obedience. We can trust our GOD, and His heart is for us. He is changing us from glory to glory for His glory as we journey with Him. This is true spiritual warfare: Finding Jesus in the struggle—He is always there.

The Heart of Jesus for You
I am intentional about you. I created you for My good pleasure in My image. Do not be afraid to dream. Your dreams are My intentions for you. I am not challenged by what you are not. Expect Me to show up. I am on your side cheering you on. I am even waving at you.

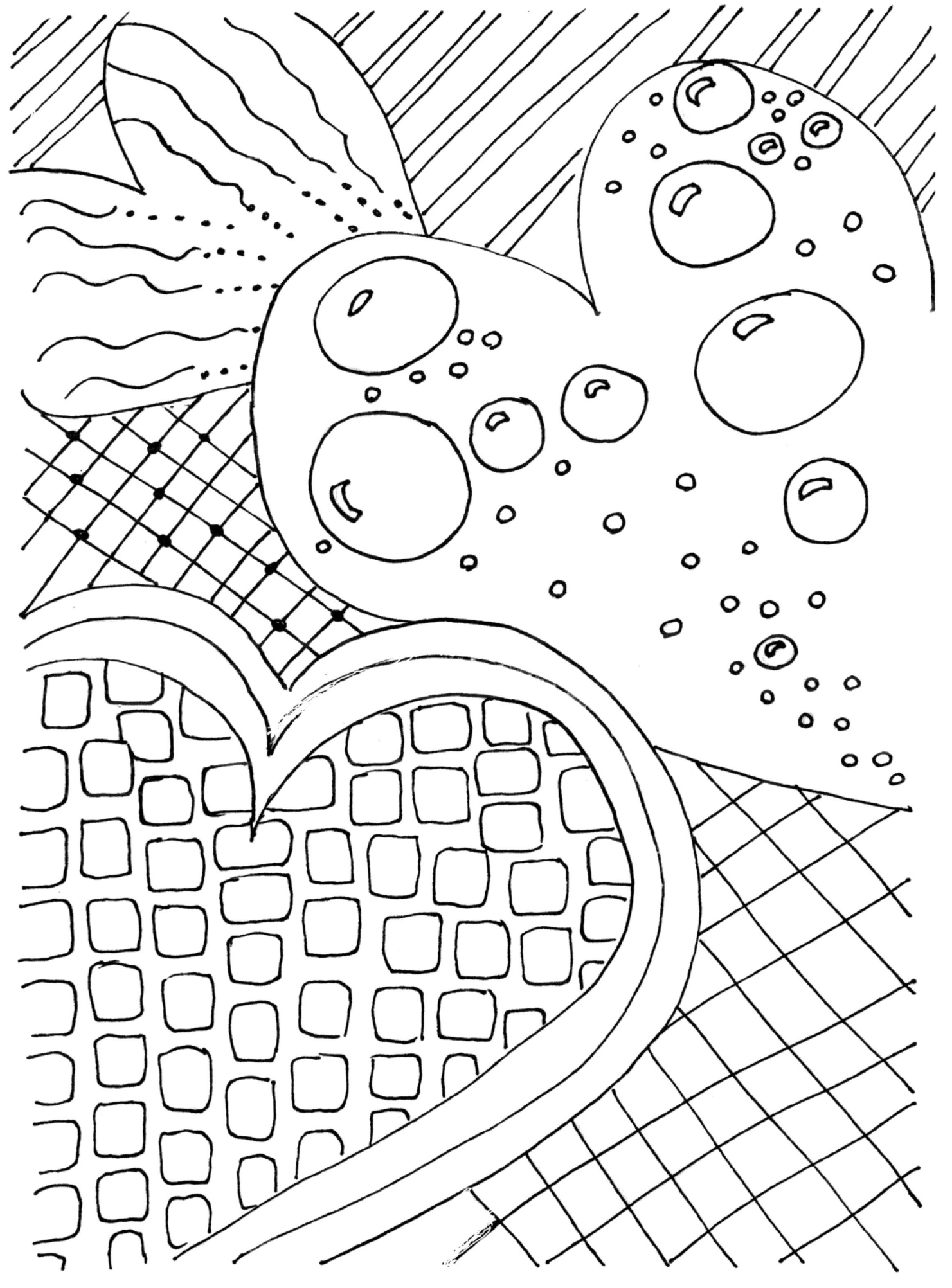

Doodle Page

HEAR THE FATHER SAYING...

FIND GRACE AND RECEIVE MERCY

*Therefore if any man be in Christ, he is a new creature:
old things are passed away; behold, all things are become new.*
2 Corinthians 5:17 KJV

For we do not have a high priest who is unable to empathize with our weaknesses, but we have one who has been tempted in every way, just as we are--yet he did not sin. Let us then approach God's throne of grace with confidence, so that we may receive mercy and find grace to help us in our time of need.
Hebrews 4:15-16 NIV

It's time to embrace the "new" you! Remember, in Christ, God only sees Jesus. Yay!! That is something to shout about. The life cycle of a butterfly is such a beautiful example of a life IN Christ. The metamorphosis life cycle is egg, larvae, pupa, and adult. One time I had started a butterfly experiment in our home. Unfortunately, due to a house flood, we had to move out temporarily to have mold remediation. When we moved back in, I stumbled across a pupa which had a thick, hard shell. At first, I was going to throw it away, but it literally began to bounce up and down and shake profusely. This went on for hours; it wouldn't stop! I knew it wasn't dead; I just needed to leave it alone. I was so excited I hadn't killed it!

I was maneuvering through some pretty traumatic events at the time, and I thought to myself, "I feel like that butterfly being beaten to death inside that shell." I researched the life of a pupa. It turns out the pupa must go through extreme pressure to emerge into a beautiful butterfly. Isn't that like life with all its struggles? Challenges can make us stronger, better people, and more like Jesus; nevertheless, we must choose to move past the pain and allow ourselves to come forth more beautiful. The length of the journey depends on our obedience to Holy Spirit. The Israelites could have passed through the wilderness in 11 days, but it took them 40 years! Let's choose the shorter route of obedience!

God is making something beautiful of our messes. The best news is that the work was finished 2000 years ago when Jesus died on that cross. Keep pressing into His loving arms. When you can't feel Him, choose to trust Him and His word. He is GOOD!

The Heart of Jesus for You
You will soar with Me when you learn to obey Me, abide in Me, and rest in My affection for YOU.

TODAY I WILL SOAR

During my quiet time one morning, I was given this acronym for soar.

S = Seek me with your whole heart.
"You shall love the Lord your God with all your heart and with all your soul and with all your strength and with all your mind, and your neighbor as yourself" (Luke10:27 ESV).

O = Overcome evil with good.
"Do not be overcome by evil, but overcome evil with good" (Romans 12:21 NIV).

A = Abide in me. "If you abide in me, and my words abide in you, ask whatever you wish, and it will be done for you" (John 15:7 ESV).

R = Rest in my affection for you.
"I have loved you with an everlasting love; Therefore with lovingkindness I have drawn you" (Jeremiah 31:3 NKJV).

This was awesome, but how was this going to pay my bills? I asked that myself. This was so life changing for my soul that I was able to focus and be more productive. My business began to thrive as I allowed Holy Spirit to heal my heart, and I kept my eyes on Jesus. God desires for us to prosper and be in health, even as our soul prospers (3 John 1:2). When we are hungry, angry, lonely, or tired, we are vulnerable to a possible attack on our emotions. It's a good time to be consciously aware of the need to guard our hearts and not take things personally.

Ask Holy Spirit if there is an area that is difficult for you to allow Him to heal. See yourself as He sees you. Choose to receive His love and meditate on the above scriptures. Remember to soak. Just sit with Him and try to not do anything. Just BE. Shutting off your mind may be difficult at first. Be patient with yourself. You will grow more and more comfortable simply *being*; eventually, you may find that you are running to this place of rest throughout your day.

Prayer
Daddy, I am here, and I want to hear you. I crawl into Your lap where I feel protected. I surrender all my distractions over to You. Show me how to simplify my life and truly SOAR with You. I commit to Your ways. Help me to partner with You as You move in and through my life. In Jesus name, amen.

A Friend Always Loves

A friend loves at all times.
Proverbs 17:17 NIV

It is so easy to allow close friends to get in the way of hearing from the BEST friend, Holy Spirit. Often, we call our friends before we ask our personal trainer for direction. It is so good to have others hold our hand, cheer us on, and even bring about correction when we need it. The key is to always have a teachable spirit. Nevertheless, no one but Holy Spirit knows the motives of our hearts. Everyone has opinions; be free today as you seek direction. Write down what comes to your heart and find scriptures that confirm what your heart is saying; then, stand on His word. Find those who will encourage you and remind you of God's words to you. He is your strength forever! Be a *"no-matter-what"* kind of person. He is teaching you endurance. It is easier to run this race with joy when you see the blessings in the gift of the present. "You keep him in perfect peace whose mind is stayed on you, because he trusts in you" (Isaiah 26:3 ESV).

As you color, consider listening to praise and worship music. Because as you Himtangle what your heart sees and feels, you are singing and dancing over your inner heart's desires and struggles. Focusing on Jesus, not circumstances, brings peace and rest to our souls.

Please remember to make one necessary change today. Holy Spirit will tell you at least one change to make sure you **SOAR** to the next level with Him. Receive the upgrade; little bits of consistency lead to great success.

What desires have yet to be fulfilled? Consider writing them down, so you can visualize them. You may even want to create a dream board or a vision board—especially if you have not done one before. It will help you to keep God's desires for you in the forefront of your mind or spark new interests in you that have been hidden in your heart. Your dreams are His intentions for you. You were uniquely created to do what only YOU can do; and no one else can do it like YOU.

<u>The Heart of Jesus for You</u>
Even in the mundane I am in you. Even if you can't feel Me, I am leading and guiding your footsteps. Look for Me in the ordinary. I am so pleased with you. Be still and know I Am God. Rest and trust Me. I love you so. (Proverbs 3:5; Psalm 46:10; Matthew 11:28)

ALL YOU NEED IS LOVE

Every country has its way of saying LOVE. It is the most used phrase universally.

French: Je t'aime.
Pronounced: Zhuh tem.
The J in Je sounds like the g in mirage. T'aime (Tem) rhymes with them.

Spanish: Te amo.
Pronounced: Tay ahm-oh.
Te amo is the more romantic version, as opposed to the more common Te quiero.

Italian : Ti amo.
Pronounced: Tee-ah-mo.
This sounds very similar to Spanish.

German : Ich liebe Dich.
Pronounced: Ish leeba dish or Ick leeba dick.
The Germans pronounce this differently in different parts of the country

Swedish: Jag älskar dig.
Pronounced: Ya ellscar dey.

Russian : Ya lyublyu tebya.
Pronounced: Ya loobloo tebya.

The world's view of love has various meanings, depending on who you ask. The Beatles hit song, *"Love Is All You Need"* was the mindset of the '60's. Americans abuse the word to say we love chocolate as well as to describe a movie. According to Merriam-Webster's dictionary, love is, "1) strong affection for another arising out of kinship or personal ties; 2) attraction based on sexual desire : affection and tenderness felt by lovers; 3) affection based on admiration, benevolence, or common interests."[1]

Nevertheless, the Word of God has different instructions:
    Agape = unconditional love described in 1 Corinthians 13
    Phileo = brotherly love when Jesus asked Peter if He loved Him 3 times after his betrayal
    Erotica = love as in a sexual relationship

To love anyone according to the Word, can only be done IN Christ. As you learn all the ways to say "I Love You" in different languages, commit the LOVE chapter (1 Corinthians 13) to memory as well. It will revolutionize your thinking and actions as you fill your love tank with God's view of love. You will learn to act through the eyes of love and not react as often in fleshly ways.

> "Love suffers long *and* is kind; love does not envy; love does not parade itself, is not puffed up; does not behave rudely, does not seek its own, is not provoked, thinks no evil; does not rejoice in iniquity, but rejoices in the truth; bears all things, believes all things, hopes all things, endures all things….
>
> "And now abide faith, hope, love, these three; but the greatest of these *is* love (1 Corinthians 13:4-7, 13 NKJV)."

---

1. https://www.merriam-webster.com/dictionary/love

The Heart of Jesus for You

As you walk with Me and talk with Me, I will tell you how to respond to those triggers that take you out of your peace. I have given you everything you need to overcome in this world. Be steadfast, steady your heart, and stay grounded in Me. You will soar to great heights when you stay focused on Me. Peter began to sink as He took his eyes off of Me; you will too. I have told you these things so you won't be surprised. You have My mind now. Stay heart felt not head strong. I love you always and forever.

Doodle Page

MY HEART HAS A HOME

My house shall be a house of prayer.
Matthew 21:13/ Mark 11:17

Don't you know your body is the temple of the Holy Spirit?
Romans 12:1-2

Our hearts are always wandering. Many scriptures talk about guarding our hearts for out of it flow the issues of life. It is the seat of our emotions. After Holy Spirit comes into us, our souls find relief as we guard our emotions. Life and all its troubles can cause our hearts much pain.

As you color these houses, consider your body as the first home, your soul as the second home, and your spirit as the third home.

You may find it helpful to write down any areas Holy Spirit is putting His finger on that He wants to heal. God reveals that which He wants to heal. Believe that He is always there for you, so freedom is around the corner. One step at a time, as you press in, your physical body will look better. You'll find your emotions are more stable as you focus on Jesus, and you'll discover that you are in constant conversation with Him. This is a happy soul: one that is surrendered to Holy Spirit. His joy abounds. Are you always happy? Not exactly, but as you count your blessings and stay thankful, you will see that you are truly a blessed individual.

As Believers, our story is shared with the world. This is why we need a Savior; this life is so temporary. Allow your heart to find a safe place in the arms of a loving Savior, receive His unconditional love, and you will be victorious!

<u>The Heart of Daddy God for You</u>
I am drawing you to a deeper walk with Me. It may feel uncomfortable. Just look to Me. Trust Me. Rest in Me. Believe all things are possible. You are safe with Me.

YOU SHALL BE SAFE

But whoever trusts in the LORD shall be safe.
Proverbs 29:25b NKJV

They didn't enter my rest because of doubt and unbelief.
Hebrews 3-4 summary

Perfect love casts out fear.
1 John 4:18

With crime on the rampage, it is easy to allow our emotions free reign and become fearful. Caring too much can become overprotective. Being cautious can become a panic attack. As you work through this design, ask Holy Spirit where the doors have been opened to fear, doubt, and unbelief. Ask Him to pour His oil into those broken places that are keeping you captive. Luke 4:18 explains why Jesus came: to set the captives free. Freedom is available because God's love is so big.

Take a few minutes and write down the areas that bring you frustration. Every emotion stems from love or anger. Even dread comes from a deep root of anger. The subtle lies we have believed, even in our childhood, can keep us from our callings. Let go. Seek God. He promises that you will find Him. It's like a game of Hide and Seek—except God never hides. Perception is so powerful. Are you focusing on the negative or the positive? He didn't give you a spirit of fear. "For God gave us a spirit not of fear but of power and love and self-control" (2 Timothy 1:7 ESV). These scriptures are powerful promises. Stand on them during your next upheaval. Jesus in you is **enough**.

Receive His love forever. Don't allow your mind to take over. We need to think about His words and what He says about us. We need to speak those words out loud. Our enemy needs to hear them and know that we are in agreement with what God says about us, our situations, and our destinies. When we resist the enemy, he has to flee. He hates the Lord's name. Stand firm, and watch God deliver you from your situation. "And let us not grow weary of doing good, for in due season we will reap, if we do not give up" (Galatians 6:9).

YOU ARE MY SUNSHINE

My BoMama, (maternal grandmother) would sing, *"You Are My Sunshine"* to all her grandchildren during our summer visits to the Tennessee Smoky Mountains. This was the highlight of my summers. Chasing after the fireflies, staying up late, making leis with marigolds, snapping peas, tromping through the rose gardens, and eating fried green tomatoes are precious memories for our family.

My sweetest memory of my grandmother is her quick trips to the gardens for flowers that she would carry to the sick in the hospital. She sauntered through the flowerbeds in her elegant alligator shoes and with rings on all of her fingers. Such a lady she was; Marjorie Rose Hollingsworth was a ray of sunshine to those she visited in the hospitals and everywhere else she went. I saw the joy she brought, and it made such an impression on my heart. I believe her spirit helped me as I have walked through my family's struggles with sickness and disease. Visiting the sick, lonely, and depressed can weigh heavy on the heart. I am asking God to make His love so real to you. I long for you to know that when you cry out to Him, He sends an angel to carry you through to the other side of your trial. Hear the Lord sing this over you: "You are My Sunshine." When you embrace what He says about you and allow your heart and head to connect, joy will come.

We have been forgiven, and His blood covers it all. Take a minute and thank Jesus. He paid our debt, so we can truly soar and live life without regrets. We are under that blood. God sees us righteous through the blood of the perfect Lamb, Jesus. He loves it when we come and surrender to Him. We don't have to compare ourselves to anyone because God sees us through the finished work of the cross of Christ. We are no longer slaves. We are children of God seated in Heavenly places with Christ.

Maybe you will find a place in your heart for the sunshine song and sing it over yourself or your children. It always brings a smile to my lips, and I hope it will to yours too.

DOODLE PAGE

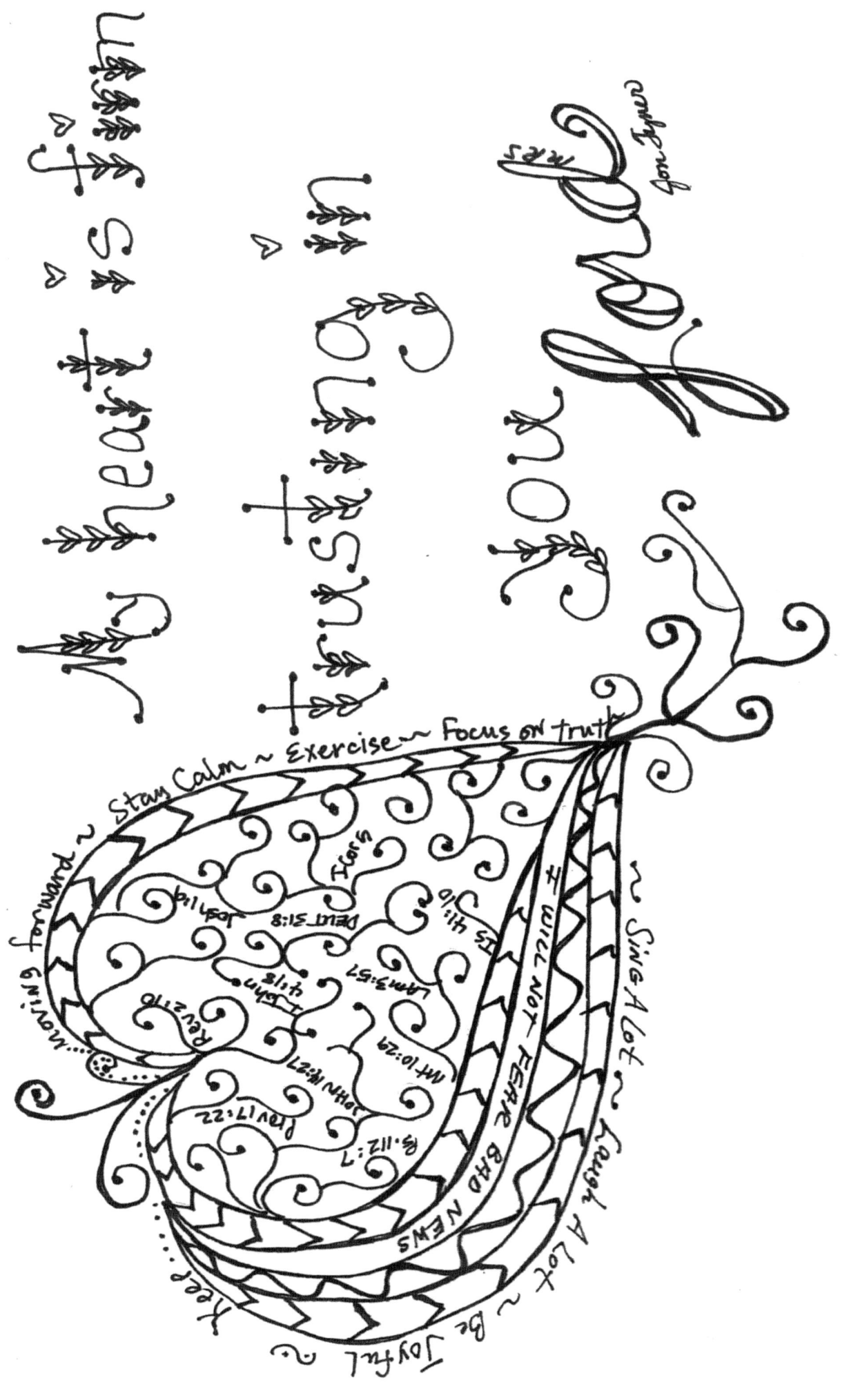

LOVE OF HOLY SPIRIT

One beautiful Sunday morning, Dr. Ted Traylor of Olive Baptist Church, Pensacola, Florida, delivered a powerful message titled, "The Love of the Holy Spirit." I created the cover for this coloring devotional during his sermon. He primarily focused on Isaiah 11:2, "And the Spirit of the Lord shall rest upon him, the Spirit of wisdom and understanding, the Spirit of counsel and might, the Spirit of knowledge and the fear of the Lord" (ESV).

The Holy Spirit was given to empower and comfort us. He gives us the fear of the Lord, guards us, refreshes us, and teaches us. Holy Spirit imparts wisdom and counsels us on our daily walk. He gives us strength, understanding, and knowledge.

When you need Holy Spirit, He is only a prayer away. You can receive help—simply ask Him. Rest in Him so that your joy may be full.

<u>The Heart of Jesus for You</u>
When I ascended into Heaven I promised you a Helper. Look to Me when you are in doubt or fear. I am always available. Don't doubt that you hear Me. You are becoming something beautiful. Enjoy the journey. Every day is a gift.

Doodle Page

love came down ♡ love came down ♡ love ... 〰 ... 〰 ... 〰 ... 〰 ... 〰 ... 〰 ...
love came down ♡ love came down ♡ love ... 〰 ... 〰 ... 〰 ... 〰 ... 〰 ...
mountain high or valley low. ♡ love

LOVE LOVE LOVE

I AM YOURS

LOVE LOVE LOVE

love came down ♡ love came down ♡ love came down ♡ love came down ♡ love came down ♡ and set me free ♡ mountain high or valley low

Words from the song, "Love Came Down" by Brian Johnson

Essential Oil suggestions for your LOVE Himtangle

Abundance = Orange, Frankincense, Patchouly, Clove, Ginger, Myrhh, Cinnamon Bark, Spruce

Acceptance = Rosewood, Geranium, Frankincense, Blue Tansy, Sandalwood, Neroli, in almond oil

Awaken = Joy, Bergamot, Ylang Ylang, Geranium, Rosewood, Lemon Mandarin, Jasmine, Roman Chamomile, Palmarosa

Forgiveness Oil = Geranium, Rosewood, Melissa, Lemon, Frankincense, Jasmine, Roman Chamomile, Bergamot, Ylang Ylang, Palmarosa, Sandalwood, Angelica, Lavender, Helichrysum, Rose, in a base of sesame seed oil

Present Time = Neroli, Spruce, Ylang Ylang, in almond oil

Build Your Dream = Sandalwood, Tangerine, Ylang Ylang, Black Pepper, Bergamot, Juniper, Anisum, Blue Tansy, Hyssop

Harmony = (Lavender, Sandalwood, Ylang Ylang, Frankincense, Orange, Angelica, Geranium, Spruce, Hyssop, Sage, Lavender, Rosewood, Jasmine, Roman Chamomile, Bergamot, Palmarosa, Rose in a base of almond oil

Believe = Idaho Balsam Fir, Rosewood, Frankincense

Joy = Bergamot, Ylang Ylang, Geranium, Lemon, Coriander, Tangerine, Jasmine, Roman Chamomile, Palmarosa, Rose

Peace and Calming = Tangerine, Orange, Ylang Ylang, Patchouli, Blue Tansy

Release = Ylang Ylang, Lavendin, Geranium, Sandalwood, Blue Tansy, in a base of Olive oil

Sara = Ylang Ylang, Lavender, Geranium, Lavender, Orange, Blue Tansy, Cedarwood, Rose, White Lotus, in almond oil

We Are a 3-Part Whole

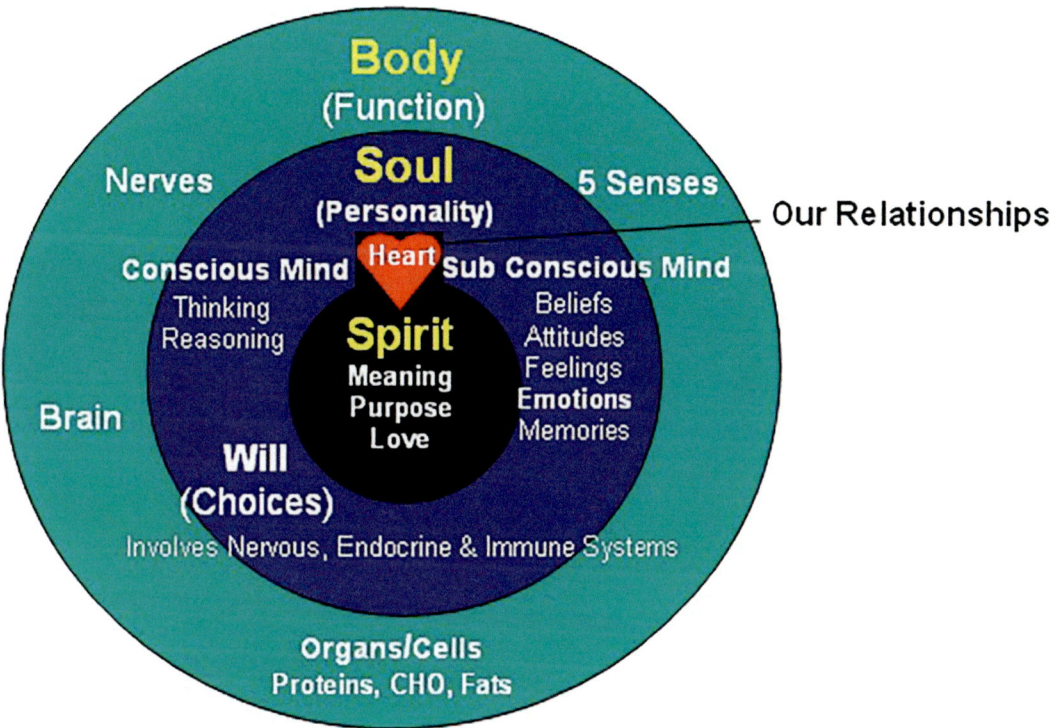

We are spirit, have a soul and live in a body

May God himself, the God of peace, sanctify you through and through. May your whole spirit, soul and body be kept blameless at the coming of our Lord Jesus Christ. 24 The one who calls you is faithful, and he will do it" (1 Thessalonians 5:23-24 NIV)

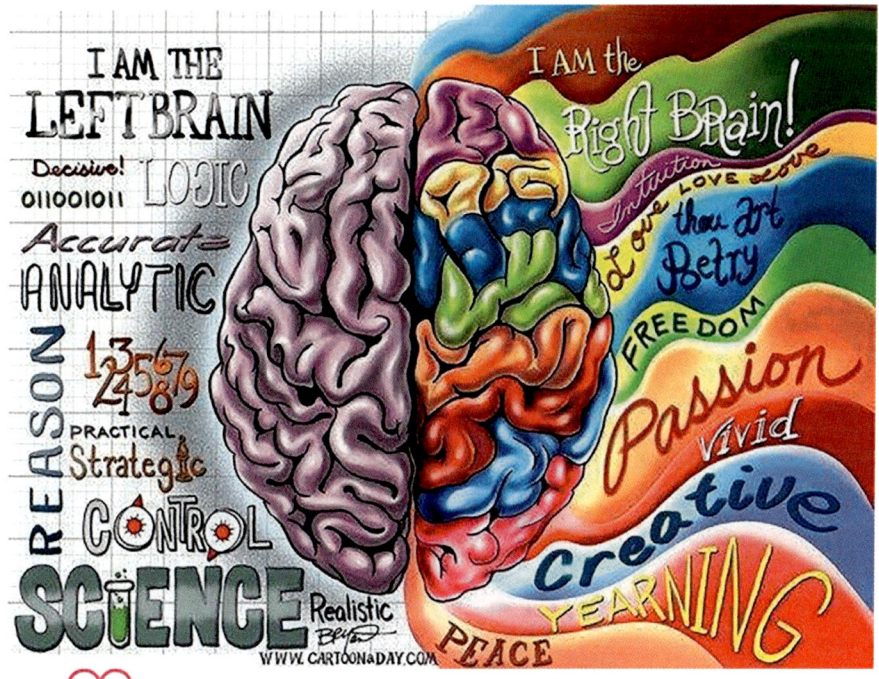

Melrose Essentials YL#1145686

1 Thessalonians 5:23-24

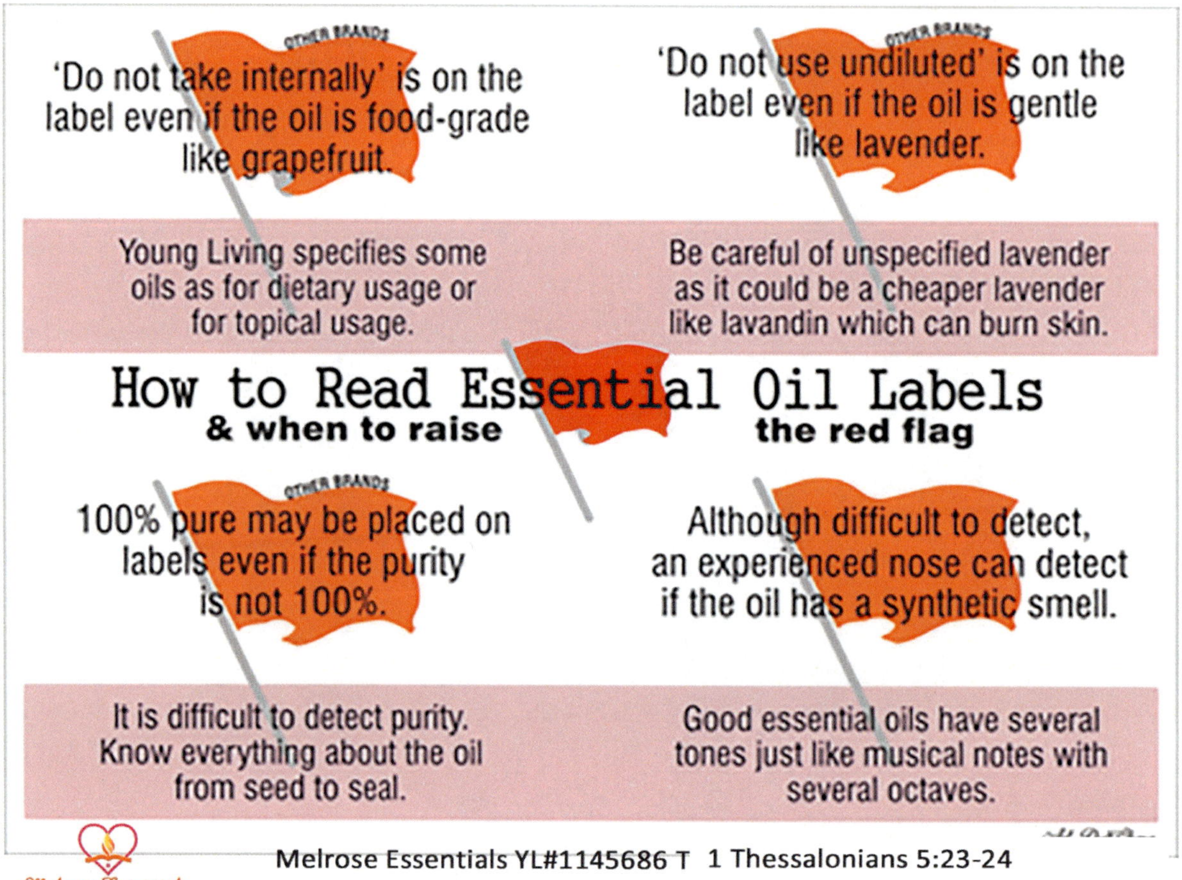

How to Read Essential Oil Labels
& when to raise the red flag

🚩 'Do not take internally' is on the label even if the oil is food-grade like grapefruit.

Young Living specifies some oils as for dietary usage or for topical usage.

🚩 'Do not use undiluted' is on the label even if the oil is gentle like lavender.

Be careful of unspecified lavender as it could be a cheaper lavender like lavandin which can burn skin.

🚩 100% pure may be placed on labels even if the purity is not 100%.

It is difficult to detect purity. Know everything about the oil from seed to seal.

🚩 Although difficult to detect, an experienced nose can detect if the oil has a synthetic smell.

Good essential oils have several tones just like musical notes with several octaves.

Melrose Essentials YL#1145686 T   1 Thessalonians 5:23-24

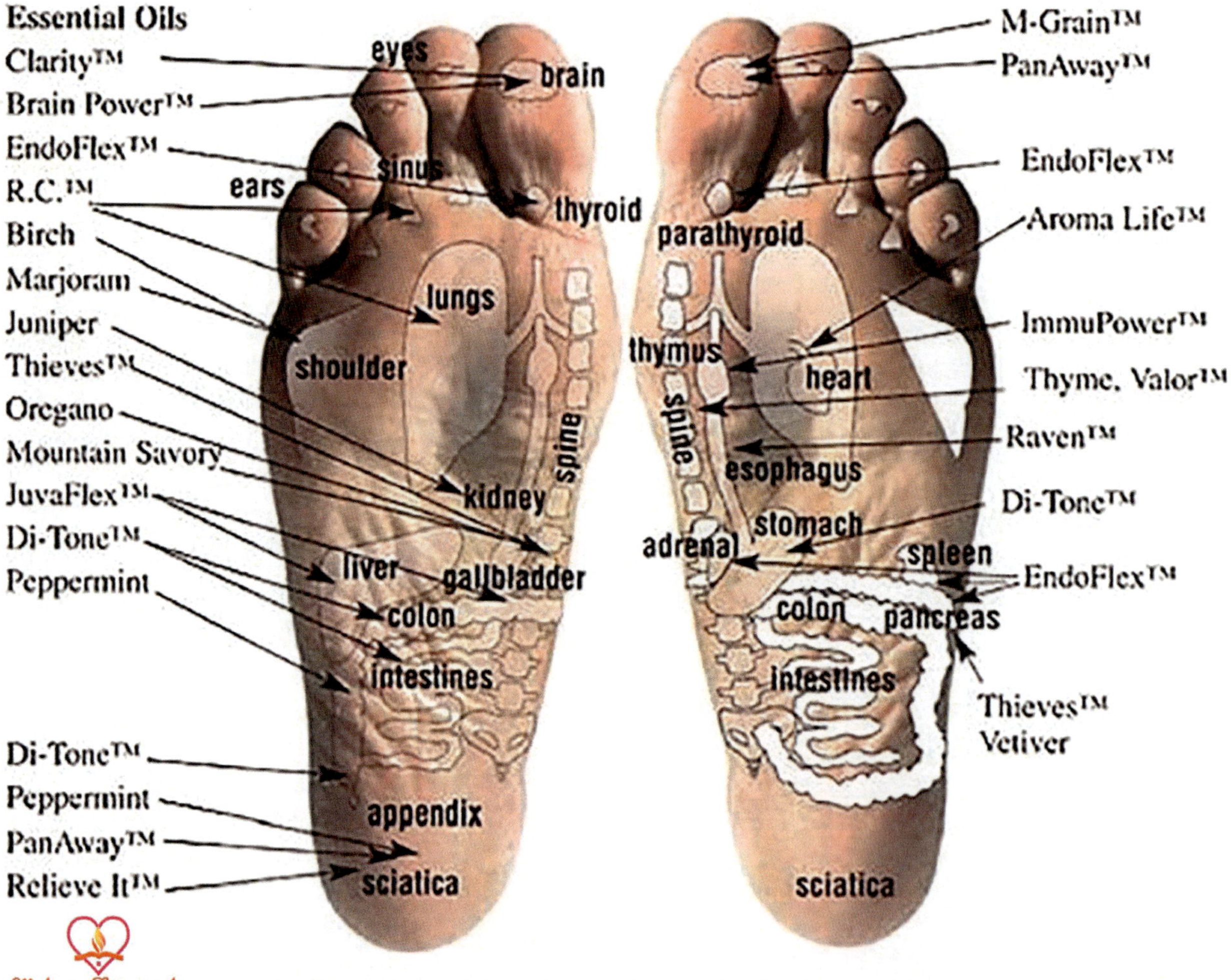

Essential Oils

Left foot:
- Clarity™ — eyes
- Brain Power™ — brain
- EndoFlex™
- R.C.™ — ears, sinus
- Birch — thyroid
- Marjoram — lungs
- Juniper
- Thieves™ — shoulder
- Oregano
- Mountain Savory — spine
- JuvaFlex™ — kidney
- Di-Tone™ — liver, gallbladder
- Peppermint — colon, intestines
- Di-Tone™
- Peppermint — appendix
- PanAway™
- Relieve It™ — sciatica

Right foot:
- M-Grain™
- PanAway™
- EndoFlex™
- Aroma Life™ — parathyroid
- ImmuPower™ — thymus, heart
- Thyme, Valor™
- Raven™ — spine, esophagus
- Di-Tone™ — stomach, adrenal
- EndoFlex™ — spleen
- Thieves™ — colon, pancreas
- Vetiver — intestines
- sciatica

Melrose Essentials YL#1145686   1 Thessalonians 5:23-24

How to use EO? FEET

*1 Safest route to the body via the large skin pores at the bottom of the feet.

*2 All the reflex points of the important organs are found at the bottom of the feet.

*3 Apply 1~3 drops of eo, rub your foot soles together. Safe, fast & convenient!

Use Thieves to fortify immune system for fall.

ImmuPower & Exodus2 are also fortifying oils.

Safe for children but please keep veg oil handy.
Use only **therapeutic-grade essential oils**.

This statement has been evaluated by the Food & Drug Administration. This product is not intended to diagnose, treat, cure, or prevent disease.

Melrose Essentials YL#1145686   1 Thessalonians 5:23-24

How to use EO? SPINE

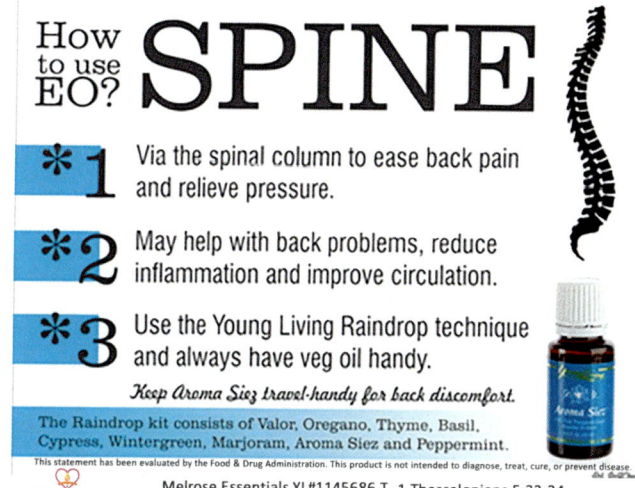

*1 Via the spinal column to ease back pain and relieve pressure.

*2 May help with back problems, reduce inflammation and improve circulation.

*3 Use the Young Living Raindrop technique and always have veg oil handy.

Keep Aroma Siez travel-handy for back discomfort.

The Raindrop kit consists of Valor, Oregano, Thyme, Basil, Cypress, Wintergreen, Marjoram, Aroma Siez and Peppermint.

This statement has been evaluated by the Food & Drug Administration. This product is not intended to diagnose, treat, cure, or prevent disease.

Melrose Essentials YL#1145686 T   1 Thessalonians 5:23-24

How to use EO? SMELL

*1 Shortest route to the body via the olfactory nerves (nose) to the brain.

*2 The brain then sends signals via the nerves to where there is pain or anxiety.

*3 Use a diffuser, smell from the cap or bottle or smell from your cupped hands.

Lemon is a top favorite!

Be cautious of synthetic or oils with additives.
Use only **therapeutic-grade essential oils**.

This statement has been evaluated by the Food & Drug Administration. This product is not intended to diagnose, treat, cure, or prevent disease.

Melrose Essentials YL#1145686   1 Thessalonians 5:23-24

How to use EO? SKIN

*1 Essential oil is absorbed transdermally via the skin pores.

*2 Some oils are gentle while others are HOT. Always keep vegetable oil handy.

*3 Allow a few mins when layering oils to achieve the benefits of each oil.

Melaleuca alternifolia is a very gentle oil.

When skin gets hot, do not flush with water which will aggravate the condition. Apply vegetable oil instead.

This statement has been evaluated by the Food & Drug Administration. This product is not intended to diagnose, treat, cure, or prevent disease.

Melrose Essentials YL#1145686 T   1 Thessalonians 5:23-24

Safety EO Reminders

Melrose Essentials *for heart and home*

What parts shouldn't you touch when you have EO?

Your eyes, your nasal membranes, no oils should be dripped into ears. Also, sensitive body parts.

What can't you use with EO?

Plastic or styropor cups, they melt. Use glass instead.

What shouldn't you touch when you have EO?

Your nail polish, your computer or cellphone keypads. The paint gets erased.

This statement has been evaluated by the Food & Drug Administration. This product is not intended to diagnose, treat, cure, or prevent disease.

Melrose Essentials YL#1145686 1 Thessalonians 5:23-24

Melrose Essentials
YL#1145686

1 Thessalonians 5:23-24

Melrose Essentials YL#1145686   1 Thessalonians 5:23-24

ESSENTIAL OIL FREQUENCIES

Oil	Frequency	Oil	Frequency	Oil	Frequency
Abundance	78 MHz	German Chamomile	105 MHz	Myrrh	105 MHz
Acceptance	102 MHz	Grounding	140 MHz	PanAway	112 MHz
Aroma Life	84 MHz	Harmony	101 MHz	Peace & Calming	105 MHz
Awaken	89 MHz	Helichrysum	181 MHz	Peppermint	78 MHz
Basil	52 MHz	Hope	98 MHz	Present Time	98 MHz
Bergamot	105 MHz	Humility	88 MHz	Purification	46 MHz
Brain Power	78 MHz	Idaho Blue Spruce	428 MHz	Raven	70 MHz
Christmas Spirit	104 MHz	Immupower	89 MHz	Ravintsara	134 MHz
Citrus Fresh	90 MHz	Inner Child	98 MHz	RC	75 MHz
Clarity	101 MHz	Inspiration	141 MHz	Release	102 MHz
Di-Gize	102 MHz	Into the Future	88 MHz	Relieve It	56 MHz
Dragon Time	72 MHz	Joy	188 MHz	Rose	320 MHz
Dream Catcher	98 MHz	Juniper	98 MHz	Sacred Mountain	176 MHz
Endoflex	138 MHz	Juva Flex	82 MHz	Sandalwood	96 MHz
En-R-Gee	106 MHz	Lavender	118 MHz	Sara	102 MHz
Envision	90 MHz	Live with Passion	89 MHz	Sensation	88 MHz
Exodus II	180 MHz	Magnify/Purpose	99 MHz	Surrender	89 MHz
Forgiveness	192 MHz	Melissa	102 MHz	Thieves	150 MHz
Frankincense	147 MHz	Melrose	48 MHz	3 Wise Men	72 MHz
Galbanum	56 MHz	M-Grain	72 MHz	Trauma Life	92 MHz
Gathering	99 MHz	Mister	147 MHz	Valor	47 MHz
Gentle Baby	152 MHz	Motivation	103 MHz	White Angelica	89 MHz

Melrose Essentials YL#1145686 1 Thessalonians 5:23-24

Vibration Frequency Chart

God-View	Life-View	Level	Log	Emotion	Process
Self	Is	ENLIGHTENMENT	700-1000	Ineffable	Pure Consciousness
All-Being	Perfect	PEACE	600	Bliss	Illumination
One	Complete	JOY	540	Serenity	Transfiguration
Loving	Benign	LOVE	500	Reverence	Revelation
Wise	Meaningful	REASON	400	Understanding	Abstraction
Merciful	Harmonious	ACCEPTANCE	350	Forgiveness	Transcendence
Inspiring	Hopeful	WILLINGNESS	310	Optimism	Intention
Enabling	Satisfactory	NEUTRALITY	250	Trust	Release
Permitting	Feasible	COURAGE	200	Affirmation	Empowerment
Indifferent	Demanding	PRIDE	175	Scorn	Inflation
Vengeful	Antagonistic	ANGER	150	Hate	Aggression
Denying	Disappointing	DESIRE	125	Craving	Enslavement
Punitive	Frightening	FEAR	75	Anxiety	Withdrawal
Disdainful	Tragic	GRIEF	75	Regret	Despondency
Condemning	Hopeless	APATHY	50	Despair	Abdication
Vindictive	Evil	GUILT	30	Blame	Destruction
Despise	Miserable	SHAME	20	Humiliation	Elimination

Created by David M Masters

Melrose Essentials YL#1145686 1 Thessalonians 5:23-24

Doodle Page

GOD LOVES YOU!

God is drawing you to Himself. He wants you to receive His free gift of salvation. Jesus wants you to receive His love and fill you with the Holy Spirit more than anything. He is the Prince of Peace and the Savior of your soul. As you talk to Him and grow in relationship, you will find that He is the lover of your soul. God will empower you and give you grace for every day. If you do not have a personal relationship with Jesus, pray the following prayer. You can experience a new life in Christ. Oh, how Jesus loves you and has an awesome plan for your life!

Dear Heavenly Father,

You loved the world so much that You sent Jesus to die for our sins; if I believe in You, I will have everlasting life. Your word says that we are saved by grace through faith as a gift from You. I cannot work or earn this. Your blood did it all for my salvation. I admit that I am a sinner, and I believe that You have forgiven me. I believe and confess with my mouth that Jesus is Your Son—the Savior of the world. I believe He died on the cross for me, paid the price for my sins, and took my place. I believe that You raised Jesus from the dead. I believe that He is now seated in Heaven praying for me. I believe that I am now a child of God. I believe that I am saved and will spend eternity with You. Help me to continually receive Your great love for me. Help me to know You and the power of Your resurrection. In Jesus name, amen.

You may want to look up the following verses either in a Bible or on https://www.biblegateway.com/:
John 3:16
Ephesians 2:8-9
1 Corinthians 15:3-4
Romans 10:9-10
Philippians 3:10
1 John 1:9
Acts 1:8
Romans 6:10-11

You are FORGIVEN. You are LOVED. You are WANTED. You are CHOSEN.

DOODLE PAGE

ABOUT THE AUTHOR
MELANIE ROSE SCHROEDER SACCOMANNO

Hi, my name is Melanie. I have been married 34 years to a wonderful man named Peter. God gave us three amazing daughters, Lauren, 30, Lindsey 27, and Leah 22. My man loves us, provides and protects us, and puts up with all this estrogen in our home by the grace of God. There will be a special bathroom in heaven for a man who lives with four women. But I will let you in on a secret: he uses more hair spray than the rest of us put together—although he may or may not admit it.

I work from home, and I homeschooled my children—ONLY out of obedience. To be honest, I didn't even know what it was 28 years ago. Homeschooling my children was a spiritual journey that forced me to press into Jesus for help. I had three main goals in life: Know God and the power of His resurrection, stay happily married, and raise Godly children.

After the last 15 grueling years, I realized that A + B wasn't equaling C. I learned I needed to press into Jesus even more to move into the next season of my life. Life is hard, but God's grace is sufficient. He anoints us and empowers for life's challenges.

My heart is that through my openness you will discover any lies you have believed that has kept you from moving forward into your destiny. After reading Donna Partow's book, *This Isn't the Life I Signed Up For*, I realized God had been draining the old oil out of me to pour in new oil. My old wine skins—old ways of thinking—weren't going to work for me anymore. Ugh! Leaning into His heart is the way to true happiness and getting refueled. God doesn't love me anymore than you. He wants to bring wholeness and refreshing to you too! Keep pressing into Him. He wants to "wow" us every day!

He has a purpose for everything He allows in our life. We are His children, and He loves us so much!

Thank you Jesus, You never give up on us!

Go forth and be all God created you to be!

If you are interested in purchasing essential oils or learning more about them, please visit: https://www.myyl.com/msaccomanno.

DOODLE PAGE